22571214R00063

Printed in Great Britain
by Amazon